Entrance to the Peace River Canyon in 1891

Hopes and dreams and kids and goods
Embark on a Canadian adventure.

Peace River Past *is a true story. It is not, however, a comprehensive history. Instead, we hope it will provide a colourful and sometimes whimsical portrait of the very real and very beautiful struggle that is a part of all of us who share the Canadian adventure — to be more than we are in a land that offers more, and demands so much.*

If, in this portrait, we can see some of the humour and the hardship, the laughter and the love, and the pride of a bygone era, then perhaps we can also catch a glimpse of our modern identity reflected back at us — in a smile or a glance, or in the ripples on the waters of a strong and quiet river.

Peace River Past

·A Canadian Adventure·

David L. Macdonald

Venture Press

Venture Press
77 Mowat Avenue, Suite 208
Toronto, Ontario
M6K 3E3

Colour renderings, map and book design by Paul Ogden

Printed and Bound in Canada by
D.W. Friesen & Sons, Altona, Manitoba

Canadian Cataloguing in Publication Data
Macdonald, David, 1947-
Peace River past

ISBN 0-919575-01-3

1. Peace River region (B.C. and Alta.) - History.
2. Peace River region (B.C. and Alta.) - History -
Pictorial works. I. Title.
FC3693.5.M33   971.23'1   C81-095080-4
F1079.P3M33

Contents

Introduction / 9

First Business *The Development of the Fur Trade / 13*

Legends *Some Early Personalities / 19*

George Dawson *A Wider Interest / 31*

Prior Claims *The Peace Country Natives / 39*

Gold *The Peace Gets a Rush / 45*

A.M. Bezanson *The Peace River Trail / 51*

Ways and Means *The Growth of Transportation / 59*

The Settlers *Moving In / 77*

Credits / 96

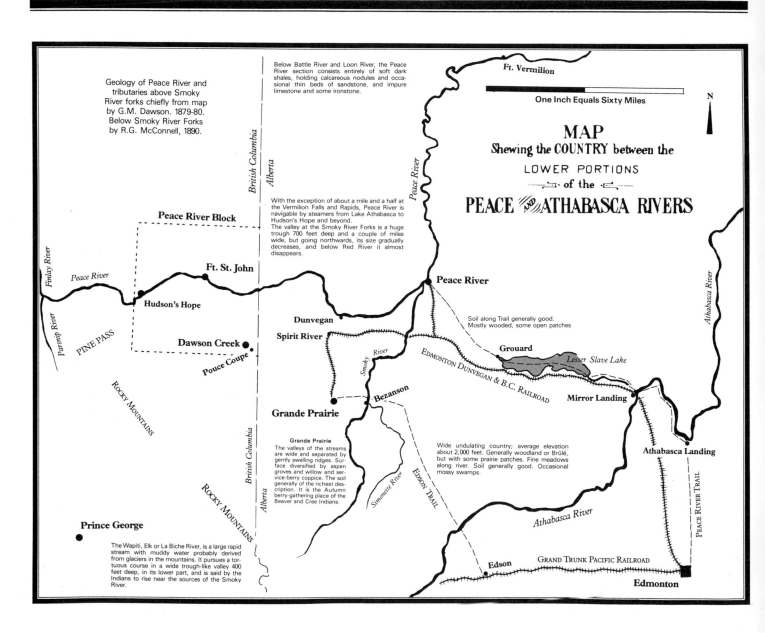

Geology of Peace River and tributaries above Smoky River forks chiefly from map by G.M. Dawson. 1879-80. Below Smoky River Forks by R.G. McConnell, 1890.

Below Battle River and Loon River, the Peace River section consists entirely of soft dark shales, holding calcareous nodules and occasional thin beds of sandstone, and impure limestone and some ironstone.

One Inch Equals Sixty Miles

N

MAP
Shewing the COUNTRY between the
LOWER PORTIONS
⊐· of the ·⊏
PEACE AND ATHABASCA RIVERS

With the exception of about a mile and a half at the Vermilion Falls and Rapids, Peace River is navigable by steamers from Lake Athabasca to Hudson's Hope and beyond.
The valley at the Smoky River Forks is a huge trough 700 feet deep and a couple of miles wide, but going northwards, its size gradually decreases, and below Red River it almost disappears.

Ft. Vermilion

Peace River

British Columbia

Alberta

Peace River Block

Ft. St. John

Finlay River

Peace River

Hudson's Hope

Parsnip River

PINE PASS

Dawson Creek

Pouce Coupe

Dunvegan

Spirit River

Smoky River

Peace River

Soil along Trail generally good. Mostly wooded, some open patches.

Grouard

Lesser Slave Lake

EDMONTON DUNVEGAN & B.C. RAILROAD

Mirror Landing

ROCKY MOUNTAINS

British Columbia

Alberta

Bezanson

Grande Prairie

Grande Prairie
The valleys of the streams are wide and separated by gently swelling ridges. Surface diversified by aspen groves and willow and service-berry coppice. The soil generally of the richest description. It is the Autumn berry-gathering place of the Beaver and Cree Indians.

Simonette River

EDSON TRAIL

Wide undulating country; average elevation about 2,000 feet. Generally woodland or Brûlé, but with some prairie patches. Fine meadows along river. Soil generally good. Occasional mossy swamps.

Athabasca Landing

PEACE RIVER TRAIL

Athabasca River

ROCKY MOUNTAINS

Prince George

The Wapiti, Elk or La Biche River, is a large rapid stream with muddy water probably derived from glaciers in the mountains. It pursues a tortuous course in a wide trough-like valley 400 feet deep, in its lower part, and is said by the Indians to rise near the sources of the Smoky River.

Edson

GRAND TRUNK PACIFIC RAILROAD

Edmonton

Introduction

The year is 1782.

Smallpox, a white man's disease, once again ravages a native population of Western Canada. The tribe to bear its scars this year is the Cree, long the favoured of the powerful Hudson's Bay Company. The Cree are in danger of losing their monopoly with the traders.

But the Hudson's Bay Company is losing a monopoly as well. Other white men encroach on their domain. All the fur-rich lands that drain into Hudson's Bay are no longer a private reserve. Scots and French Canadians — soon to call themselves the North West Company — make trade alliances with another band of Indians, the Beaver, a tribe that has traditionally been intimidated by the fiercer and better armed Cree.

Now armed with the latest in European weaponry, and with their adversary suffering the smallpox epidemic, the Beaver approach the banks of the river that has been the limit of their territory. Here they marshal their courage and incite their braves. The river is crossed and the two tribes collide in war.

When sufficient damage is inflicted by both sides to allow for a respectable truce, the two bands meet on the banks of the river that has divided them. A pipe is smoked.

The great river has run through the lives of many others in the ensuing two hundred years. For the Cree and for the Beaver, and for the pipe they smoked between them, they have called the river Peace.

The Peace River Country occupies some 25,000 square miles, or 65,000 square kilometres. It is somewhat smaller than Scotland, and to the same extent, larger than Nova Scotia. It is isolated; cut off from the Pacific by the Rockies, and from the Prairies by a dense corridor of non-arable forest. It is also the most northerly agricultural district on the continent.

Because of its location, the Peace River Country stood virtually unknown long after the sod had been turned on the rest of the Canadian prairies. It was still a part of the great northern wilderness, the domain of fur traders and Indians who lived beyond the frontiers

Tribal pride confronts the lens;
A way of life is caught on film
And quickly left behind.

of the National Consciousness.

The story of the Peace River Country begins with the people who knew it first. It follows the traders, both Indian and White, who made a home in the wild environment. It tells of the explorers and the surveyors who learned the land anew, and passed their knowledge to the outside world.

The story moves through the prospectors, who measured the value of the new land from an old world standard, and the developers, who saw it not as it was, but as it might be.

Then it becomes the story of the pioneers, the men and women who, when all was said and done, had to move in with the new land, had to learn to live with it, and to love it.

Oh yes, it is also the story of a river, and as all who live by rivers know, a river is the story of adventure!

First Business

Well into the Nineteenth Century, the development of Canada still followed the development of the fur trade. Nowhere was this more evident than in the fur-rich Peace River Country.

As motivation for development, the fur trade was unique. On the one hand, it was a cruel and reckless occupation which sacrificed ever greater numbers of animals to the satisfaction of an elitist demand for luxury. The salons of Europe were far removed from the lakes and rivers of Canada, and as animal life became depleted, the response was expediency in trapping methods, and expeditions to ever more remote territory.

But it was also an industry in which the Native had the upper hand. In much of the rest of the New World, the Native American was met with hostility, greed, and ignorance. The White Man was a soldier, a fortune hunter or a settler. The Indian was in the way. This was not the case with the fur trade, especially as it extended to the Northwest. Here the Native's first contact with the world of the White Man was through a fur trader — a man of commerce — who understood the long-term importance of developing healthy relations, and was not interested in altering the environment.

In return for furs, the Indians received more than just the coloured beads that sold New York. To woolens and heavy blankets, kettles and pots and pans from Europe, and foodstuffs from Lower Canada were added rifles and shot and metal traps to facilitate the trade. Considering the thousands of miles traveled to reach the Natives, the method of travel, and the bulk of the trade goods, it was considered fair exchange for the furs that in previous times were often discarded, the animal being hunted largely for its food value. The Indians' good health was important to the fur trader, and for this reason there was not the abuse of alcohol so prevalent at other times and in other places.

Nor was there much social contact. The White Man came once a year, or else contained himself at a trading post. The Natives were given room and time to adjust to the new life of Europe. If, in later times, the Canadian Indian has been found "in the way of progress," at least in the fur years he was part of it, and could benefit from it.

•●

The Company of Adventurers Trading into Hudson's Bay — the very name conjures up romance, though romance was not mentioned in the charter which Charles II gave to a group of well-connected Londoners in the year 1670. It gave them absolute domain in all the land that drains into Hudson Bay, an area larger than Europe. To those commercial gentlemen of the City of London, the term adventure referred to speculation — financial speculation.

So it was that a company of speculators, people who

would never consider, even for a moment, an icy voyage on the North Atlantic to visit their domain, became masters of a great part of the New World, and through their agents, introduced what is now Western Canada to the wisdom and the ways of civilization.

As an introduction, it was basic. All those lands that drained into Hudson Bay went unexplored, while the Company's ships sailed into the Bay each year and were met by the Indians from across the North — even to the Rockies — and the trade was made.

For one hundred years little changed within the Company, but around it a country was starting to take shape. It was a country that belonged to England and it was becoming difficult for the Company to justify

The trading post and the main item of trade.

its monopoly to a government advocating free trade.

The profitability of that trade encouraged others who were able to claim the ordinary rights of British subjects to compete. They made their headquarters in Montreal, hired French Canadians — descendants of the Voyageurs — and followed the old routes of the Voyageurs through the Great Lakes and into the West. In 1776 they joined forces, and called themselves the North West Company.

It was a partnership of individualists, the North West Company, and there were few rules. Men like Simon McTavish, the Frobishers, and Peter Pond were content to make their own laws. Pond was twice involved in "scuffles" with Hudson's Bay Company men and both of those Hudson's Bay men died as a result.

Of necessity, these men became explorers, in the sense that they followed paths that no White Man trod before them. Where the old Company was named for adventure, this new one was committed to it — none more so than its most illustrious partner, Alexander Mackenzie.

> *"This I consider as the highest and Southernmost source of the Unjigawah or Peace River ...which empties itself into the Frozen Ocean."*

In 1793 no others could say this; no others had made such a voyage. A few weeks later he put his mark on a rock on the Pacific Coast:

> *"Alex Mackenzie, From Canada, By Land"*

and became the first person to travel across North America north of Mexico.

He was a hard-nosed and outspoken Scot, possessed of a somewhat rugged humility:

> *"I was led, at a very early period of life, by commercial views, to the country Northwest of Lake Superior...and being endowed by Nature with an inquisitive mind and enterprising spirit; possessing also a constitution and frame of body equal to the most arduous*

Sir Alexander Mackenzie

undertakings…I not only contemplated the practicality of penetrating across the continent of America, but I was confident in my qualifications as I was animated by the desire to undertake the perilous enterprise."

Strong words for a Canadian hero. They would have better suited the American climate, where Mackenzie would have lived had not the Revolution forced his royalist family to spirit the youth to Montreal, and apprenticeship in the fur business.

There was little romance in the relationship between Mackenzie and Canada.

"I think it unpardonable in any man to remain in this country who can afford to leave it."

In the interests of the fur trade he opposed the settlement of the West, and described the wilderness as a dreadful hardship — not the least endearing — only to be endured.

It was for the world a first glimpse of the Peace Country, and for the Natives of the Peace, it was often a first glimpse of the White Man, and his ways. In all his exploration, Mackenzie never resorted to violence, even though he was often overwhelmed by inquisitive and sometimes hostile reception committees. Throughout his adventures he was aided with provision and advice from tribes that had never seen nor heard tell of the White Man.

Richard "Dick" Secord got his start trading furs with the Indians, but he found a much more lucrative pastime in buying up their land scrip. For this purpose he carried with him suitcases full of cash in small denominations. He and his partner became millionaires.

Mackenzie formed opinions:

"They (the Missionaries) should have begun their work by teaching some of the useful arts which are the inlets of knowledge, and lead the mind, by degrees, to objects of higher comprehension...Agriculture should have been the first thing introduced. It attaches the wandering tribe to that spot where it adds so much to their comfort; while it gives to them a sense of lasting prosperity...instead of the uncertain hope of the chase...The Canadian Missionaries should have been content to improve the morale of their own countrymen so that by meliorating (uplifting) their character and conduct, they would have given a striking example of the effects of religion in promoting the comforts of life..."

Mackenzie possessed a vision that would span the continent to rest on the Pacific. He could see a day when Western Canada would trade with the Orient, something he advocated long before its time. But it was also a vision that encompassed the problems he encountered on his journey, and saw for them a passage as well.

Canada often fails to recognize her heroes readily; nor does she listen to them closely when they speak.

Mackenzie's exploits added prestige to the image of his company, and the company added a network of trading posts throughout the Peace Country. By the early 1800's, the North West Company consistently outproduced the Hudson's Bay Company, and profits slipped disastrously for the older concern, so much so that dividends were suspended back in London.

The solution, from the Hudson's Bay point of view, presented itself with Lord Selkirk's Red River Colony — a block of land along the Assiniboine and Red Rivers settled by Scottish and Irish of agricultural background and donated by the Hudson's Bay Company.

From the Company's point of view, the settlement made sense. It provided them with the provisions and manpower they would need at the gateway to the West (which all agreed held their future) and it stood in the way of the competition.

Basically, the North West Company saw the settlement in much the same light. They responded by sponsoring a group of Metis to attack the settlement. Twenty-two settlers were killed.

The Hudson's Bay Company dispatched their agents to Fort Vermilion in the North Peace to try to develop some of that lucrative country. But the North West Company felt it was their own. When the Bay men ran out of food in this alien environment, the competition refused to come to the rescue, and even counselled the Natives to do likewise. Sixteen Bay agents died of starvation before the winter was over.

Charges were met by countercharges. As the traders were the only legal authority in the wilderness, arrest and deportation to Montreal was a favourite weapon of both sides. The North West played host in those days to the fiercest commercial competition in the Country's history. All sighed relief with the merger of the two companies in 1821 and the return to normalcy, under the banner of The Bay.

But the North West Company was not through. Its traders had learned quickly the secrets of the Athabasca and the Peace. They brought to the merger this knowledge, and also their vitality. The Scottish influence in the Company of Adventurers persists.

The fur trade carried on throughout the reign of Victoria, but with the advent of the new century, it became impossible to preserve the traditional ways. There was a new wave breaking on the land — a wave of settlement. When it was no longer practical to oppose it, the Hudson's Bay Company welcomed a new set of partners — a new company of adventurers — the Pioneers of the Peace!

Legends

There was gold in the Peace. Finds there were never spectacular, the way they had been in California, the Cariboo, and were to be in the Klondike, but successful placer operations began in the 1860's at the headwaters of the Peace, and lasted well over twenty years.

The hub of activity was on the Omineca and its tributary, Germansen Creek. In 1871 there were twelve hundred miners at the Germansen Camp, and a small but permanent townsite was constructed, complete with post office and saloon. Being so isolated, the town was poorly serviced, and provisions were often impossible to procure at any price. By all accounts Germansen was not a comfortable proposition.

Over the years, activity diminished. There was not enough "quick money" to alleviate the hardships, and all but the stubborn pulled out. Germansen became a ghost town. The "Gold Rush" on the Peace provided a more important contribution to the development of the region than the hasty construction of a soon forgotten townsite might indicate, for it attracted an unusual

breed of men. They were variously known as loners, as gamblers, and as drifters. But these were also men who could walk the thin edge of security, and carry freedom to new limits. They answered the river's call to adventure in their own unique ways.

While most of the prospectors moved on, some found it to their liking to remain. Their adventures have become part of the history of the river. A few are described below.

Pete Toy

It all happened a hundred years ago, just a few miles up the Finlay River — a few miles from where it joins the Parsnip to form the Peace. In those days there was gold to be had in the Peace. If the legend of Pete Toy pans true, there may still be.

Pete Toy was born in Cornwall, England, and came to the New World about 1850. It is probable that Pete, like so many of his profession and era, learned his skills

In the years after Pete Toy's time, it was no longer possible to live off the gold on the river banks. The owner of this cabin may have augmented his earnings by supplying cordwood to the ever hungry river steamers.

in the gold fields of California, and when they closed, that he moved north, through the Cariboo, and eventually to the Peace. He arrived in the Peace in '58, and found gold in that same year, staking a claim he would work for the rest of his life.

Now if, perchance, there were some who thought the North no place for a man named Toy, these were soon set straight. With his large and powerful frame and uncommon wisdom in the ways of survival, Pete Toy was better suited than most to the strenuous life of the Northern Wilderness.

In the years that followed his arrival, the name of Toy became synonymous with a certain rugged hospitality. It found many grateful recipients among Native and newcomer alike — among trappers and panners, officials of the Hudson's Bay Co. and even the occasional official of Government.

His claim had proved worth the staying, and Pete built for himself (his Native bride as well, some say) the only permanent dwelling for many miles in any direction. In the summer months he worked his claim, and in the winter he hunted and trapped, acting as guide to those in need of direction, and host to those in need of comfort.

It was in these last two capacities that Pete Toy came in contact with the distinguished explorer and chronicler of Canadiana, Major Wm. Butler. During a brief stay in Toy's cabin, Butler became fond of his host, and wrote with evident respect for his fellow Englishman, though it perplexed him how so sensitive a man as Toy could endure the loneliness of the wilderness.

Butler recalled a request given him by Toy: "And you're going back to England. You're really going to see the old land! Maybe you'd go to Cornwall? Well, if you should meet an old couple of the name of Toy down there, just say to them that you saw their son Pete — him as left them twenty years ago, and tell them that they were as fresh in his mind as the day he last saw them."

Butler never recorded a meeting with the elder Toys, but if he found it hard to understand their son's motivation, it was simple — Pete Toy was taking four ounces of gold from his claim every working day. He did this consistently for more than ten years, and it seemed to be enough to satisfy him.

But there were furs as well. As the river froze each winter, Toy would take to the forest, snow shoes and rifle with him, and return with another fortune. If this were not enough, he also maintained a trade with the local Natives, who came to trust and rely on this strange paleface.

The profits from fur alone were enough to keep Pete Toy provided for — especially in the manner he chose to live. It is likely that in the time he stayed in the Peace, he never ventured into the "outside." The scattered trading posts provided all his needs, and the hundreds of pounds of gold he took from the river bank may well be cached along that bank. Perhaps he planned to trade them later for the gentleman's life in England, or perhaps he really had no use for them after all.

It was during the Spring break-up of '74 they found his canoe, floating upside down near the mouth of the Black Canyon of the Omineca. Then they recalled that no one had seen Pete Toy during the previous Winter. As it happened, no one ever saw him again.

There may well be, where the Finlay and the Parsnip meet to form the Peace, a hidden place — a caché of gold worth millions. Until the day it is uncovered by some lucky treasure hunter, that fortune belongs to the land of the Mighty Peace, and to the legend of Pete Toy!

Dan Williams

Once the pace of gold mining slowed, the Peace River gold miners had to find other means of support, and they were suited to few occupations. One that seemed to fit was the fur trade.

Since the great merger of 1821, the Hudson's Bay Co. had enjoyed a monopoly within the Peace. The miner turned trader was an imposition, and as he was willing to travel extensively to reach the Natives, he developed as well that unmistakeable aura of trouble — much like the men of the North West Co. had a century before.

But the fur trade was an organized endeavour in the last decades of the 1800's, and the Hudson's Bay Co. controlled it. To entertain the wrath of the trading post

The Hudson's Bay post at Fort Saint John in 1891. There doesn't seem to be much left of Mr. Williams' cabin.

manager was a foolish and sometimes dangerous pursuit. Disgruntled would-be traders swore that they had been sold their provisions on one provision only — that they agreed to quit the trade. Of course, the prospector is a stubborn character by nature...

He was a cook and a miner, a guide and a trapper, a prisoner and a pioneer. Some said that he was a thief, and that he had been a murderer. In any case he was Fort St. John's first settler, and his name was Daniel Williams. He was known as Nigger Dan.

Williams was born in Napanee, Ontario, it seems, and came West with Captain Palliser. He was the expedition's cook. But this somewhat limiting profession was soon abandoned for the more adventurous occupation of gold miner. After picking up a few pointers on the Omineca, Williams arrived in Fort St. John in 1869. He built a cabin on the north side of the river — directly opposite the Hudson's Bay Co. post. He staked his claim here, planted his vegetables, and settled in.

During the winter months Williams hired out as guide, or else went off trapping to return in the spring for his gold and his garden. During one such routine winter (1872-3) the Hudson's Bay Co. decided to move its trading post back to the north side of the river. When Williams floated home that spring he found a new Hudson's Bay Co. compound nearing completion, right next door to his own establishment, and occupying land he considered to be his own.

The Hudson's Bay Co. manager was a young man named Kennedy, and he was not prepared for the wrath of the outraged miner. One morning Kennedy found the following note on his door:

April 12
Kenedy I hear by
Worne you that com and Gett your
persnol property if any you
have got of my prmeesis In 24 hours and then keep
away from me because I shal Not betrubbld nor
trod on
only by her most Noble
Majesty
Government
"D.T. Williams"

Unfortunately for Williams, the aforementioned Major Butler happened to be a guest at the post at the time. Besides causing Dan's letter to be published for all the English speaking world to read, Butler acted in his capacity as Justice of the Peace for Rupert's land and the North West Territories, and although he refused to rule on Dan's claim, he did forbid either side the use of or threats of violence.

Butler seemed to be of the impression that the cabin had not been used for some years, yet others who traveled in the area mention Williams and his cabin as if they were one. He also made light of William's writing skills and sense of propriety. Yet to be black and to be able to write, and to be able to demand recognition of one's presence — it took courage in 1870 — even in the Peace.

The battle went on. The Hudson's Bay Co. post was completed as planned, and over the next few years Williams complained bitterly that horses and dogs were allowed to trample over his garden when approaching the trading post. The Company complained that many horses and dogs were found shot.

For six years the controversy raged. Williams was classified "unbalanced," yet he remained steadfast while his rival Kennedy was transferred out of the area due to the strain. So was Kennedy's replacement. Finally in 1879 they took Williams to Fort Saskatchewan to stand trial for disturbing the peace, and because the new post manager claimed he had been shot at.

One account of the trial has Williams being defended by a fellow miner named "Banjo Mike." Apparently Mike was able to get Williams off the more serious charge of attempted murder with the following eloquence: "Gentlemen, had Dan Williams the slightest intention of harming Mr. McKinley, he (McKinley) would not be here today to tell you the amusing little story, whereby he gives you credit for some sense of humour without paying you much of a compliment for intelligence!"

Williams spent a few months in jail, after which his personal history becomes unclear. Some claimed he was hanged at Fort Saskatchewan. Others insist he headed out prospecting with a partner, and that he died of natural causes. No matter how it was accomplished, Dan Williams' passing left the Hudson's Bay Co. relieved of one of its most persistent adversaries. It left the Peace with one less pioneer — one who had come there to find space and dignity — one of the most spirited and colourful of them all.

Razor and whisker confront each other
In Sunday's weekly battle.

Twelve-foot Davis

To operate independently as a fur trader in the Peace Country required capital and resources, especially as the nineteenth Century drew to a close. The Hudson's Bay Co. was not interested in supplying the articles of the trade to competitors. It was hard enough for the independents to purchase necessities for their own survival. Most of those who attempted the trade as an alternative to the gold fields soon gave up or sold out to the large companies.

A few prospered: Those who had the initial capital to bring in supplies over the mountains (usually from Quesnel) and the resource of character to provision themselves adequately for the future. These were not qualities generally associated with "The Boys," the veterans of the gold fields. When these qualities met with an adventurous spirit and a generous heart, they provided the world with a truly unusual individual.

Such a man was Twelve Foot Davis. He came from Vermont, Mr. Henry Fuller Davis, and he learned his mining skills in California. When it came time to move north to the Cariboo, he was too late — all the good claims had been staked, and newcomers were working for wages.

Patience is golden too.

The legal claim limit in the Cariboo was 100 feet. Davis preferred not to throw in with someone else, so he undertook a little private survey. When the miners had packed up for the night, Davis would wander up and down Williams Creek, measuring all the good claims. Eventually he found what he wanted — two claims that measured a total of two hundred and twelve feet. He moved in between them and staked his own claim, thereby earning for himself a small fortune, and a new name.

When Davis entered the Peace Country he was among the first of the miners there, but by then it seems that the gold had lost some of its attraction for him. He adopted the new profession of fur trader and this he practised for most of the next forty years. With money saved from the gold fields he was able to finance an annual "outfit" of trade goods, first over the mountains from Quesnel, and later, with the coming of the railway, through Edmonton.

Davis' outfit was appreciated not only by the Indians who traded with him, but also by the independents who came to rely on him as their only line of supply. Almost without exception, contemporary accounts of travel in the Peace Country make mention of assistance, needed and obtained from Twelve Foot Davis.

He built trading posts all along the river, at one time or another, from the headwaters in the Rockies all the way to Fort Vermilion, moving farther north as the Indian families became scarcer in the South.

At Fort Dunvegan he was remembered for his knack with pastry and pumpkins grown in the mission garden. His pies (the result of a long-ago stint as a chef in Boston) earned him fame up and down the river. He was also remembered fondly for the fact that throughout his business career, he never learned to read. In Ft. Vermilion, the Reverend Garrioch observed that "Perhaps it was no great harm that Mr. Davis was uneducated, for thereby his kindness got the better of his smartness."

The Twentieth Century found Davis still travelling his route — still going down to Edmonton for supplies. But now he was eighty years old. He was crippled and nearly blind, and had to be carried from cart to canoe. It was no longer an age of fur and gold in the Peace Country, and as the Indians were, so the old-timer was, out of place. On a return trip from Edmonton, Davis collapsed and died at Bishop Grouard's Mission on the Lesser Slave.

There was a nun at the mission who nursed Davis there. She asked him if he were afraid to die (no doubt assuming the grizzled character to be not of the heavenly sort). Davis replied:

"No Miss, why should I be afraid to die?...I always kept open house for all travellers — all my life...I ain't afraid to die."

He was buried at Grouard in 1900, and his grave was later removed to a spectacular site high above the place where the Smoky meets the Peace, at the town of Peace River. It was done in honour of his own request, and his contribution to the life of the Peace.

Stalwarts of the survey repose at camp;
A young sailor dreams of far-off lands.

George Dawson

Among those to whom have fallen the honours, and the obligations of discovery in this country, few have been as observant or as dedicated, and certainly none has been as unlikely as George M. Dawson, after whom are named Dawson City and Dawson Creek.

In 1871 British Columbia joined Confederation, and all at once Ottawa's dominion extended across a continent. But it was a Dominion of uncharted wilderness, stretching from Winnipeg to the Rockies, reaching how far south no one knew, and how far north no one cared. It was agreed, by those who had the greatest stake in the new land — by London and Washington — that a boundary must be established, and a comission was set up for this purpose.

The result of that Boundary Commission, the 49th parallel, was unpopular with almost everyone, as most compromise is, but it gave to Canada one thousand miles of border, and a better understanding of what those miles entailed. To George Dawson, the young geologist-botanist attached to the Commission, it gave the first hint of a life rich in service to his country — especially its Western regions. It was a life he was determined to live, despite what many thought were insurmountable odds.

Life must provide unending possibility to the lad of ten whose interests run to science and adventure, and whose father is president of McGill College in Montreal. Even from earlier times in Nova Scotia, George had looked forward to a career based on exploration and discovery — both priorities to the Victorian Colonial.

But in that tenth year the seemingly robust lad collapsed — the victim of some unknown virus or disease. For months he lay paralyzed, semi-conscious, close to death. It was understandable that the family was overjoyed when George finally began to show some limited improvement. The elder Dawson mapped out a life of seclusion and study for the invalid son all thought lucky to be alive.

George thought differently. A determination was

Far on the Western river lay
Like molten gold, the dying day.
Far to the east the waters glide
Till lost in twilight's swelling tide;
While all around on either hand,
Spread the broad and silent tree-clad land;
And in the distance far and blue
Long swelling mountains close the view.

VERSE AND ORIGINAL PHOTOGRAPH OF PINE PASS BY G.M. DAWSON

"Her Majesty's North American Boundary Commission"
The Commissioner, Captain Cameron, sits third from left.
Dawson stands out.

born and nurtured in these years — a determination that would drive survey crews relentlessly across a continent and outdistance the hardiest of trail-blazers, to go where none had gone before.

Physical growth had ceased. George Dawson never stood taller than a ten year old child, and as he grew older, he became increasingly hunch-backed. But the young man looked inward, and there sustained a growth which attained its first measure of achievement as a scholar at McGill, and then in London at the School of Mines, where Dawson met with the most knowledgeable men of his time in the subjects of geology, minerology, and anthropology. He graduated first in his class.

Back home, Dawson's newly acquired knowledge was needed. The Hudson's Bay Co. had given up its claim to all the lands west of Ontario and north of the U.S. There were stirrings in certain quarters in Washington for annexation. Ottawa had promised B.C. there would be a railway to the Coast. Yet despite all these pressures, almost nothing was known of this awesome mass of land.

Dawson joined the Boundary Commission as geologist. While the other members surveyed and mapped, it was his responsibility to record and evaluate the geological potential of an area of 240,000 square miles — a task that would later result in a highly informative and widely read report on Western Canada. This report would, in part, become the basis for future federal immigration policy on the Prairies. At the same time, Dawson supplied the British Museum with

numerous species of hitherto unknown animal life which he collected in his travels. It was the beginning of a routine he would follow for the rest of his life.

After the work of the Boundary Commission was completed, Dawson received an appointment to the Geological Survey of Canada of which he eventually became director. From this time on his work became more centred about Northern B.C. and the Peace River Country. Sides were being drawn up and support enlisted for the different rail routes through the Rockies. Dawson came out strongly in favour of a Northern route, and recommended the early settlement of the Peace Country. Although there was considerable doubt in official minds as to the agricultural

Meeting of minds at "Fort Misery" (Fort Macleod). Dawson stands in centre.

potential of the region, Dawson never doubted it:

"The soil is everywhere fertile and susceptible to cultivation...the grass in some places is as high as the horses bellies and is already ripe and turning brown at the tops. The agricultural value of the Peace Country...is great."

Reporting for the Department of Agriculture in 1883 he states, with regard to the Grande Prairie region:

"The soil is magnificent; it is watered by beautiful streams, and it is altogether one of the most attractive countries in a state of nature I have ever seen."

It was not enough. The C.P.R. had, some years previously, rumbled through Calgary and both the Grand Trunk Pacific and the Canadian Northern would choose Edmonton and the Yellowhead Pass as their best route west.

As well as with agricultural potential, Dawson also tempted many an Eastern imagination with reports of great coal deposits and the forecast of industrial development. But until the railways came, settlement and development of the Peace would have to wait.

Dawson spent as much time as possible in the field. In 1879 he travelled well over 2,000 miles, by pack-train, canoe, and foot. He crossed the Rockies from the west through the Pine Pass, and explored much of what was then unknown Peace Country.

Yet recognition found him even in this remote setting. On the death of Dr. Selwyn he became director of the Geological Survey, and in the years just prior to his death was elected president of the Geological Society of America, and the Royal Society of Canada. A testimonial to Dr. Dawson's achievements was printed in the Victoria Colonist in 1897, after he had visited that city.

"Among the many distinguished visitors...by whose presence Victoria has been honoured... none holds a higher or more deserved place in the esteem of Canadians than George M. Dawson. In one sense he is the discoverer of Canada, for the Geological Survey, of which he has been the chief, has done more than all other agencies combined to make the potentialities of the Dominion known to the world... He can look back at it (his work) with the profound satisfaction that comes from the knowledge that his judgement on points of extreme interest has been justified by events...when he anticipates great mineral developments in parts of the Province (the Peace) that are as yet unexplored, we feel almost as if such development were guaranteed. Canada possesses in Dr. Dawson, a public servant the value of whose service can never be overestimated. That a long career may be before him is the hope of all, for we all know how much that means to the Dominion."

It was not to be a long career. In 1901, at the age of fifty-three, the relentless drive took its toll, and Dawson's strength gave out.

Perhaps the most fitting testimonial to Dawson's achievements is to be found in the name that was given him by the Indians he came in contact with. They called him Skookum Tum Tum — the Brave and the Cheerful One!

No mark, no memory left behind.
The everlasting sea, the wind – flow on.
CLOSING LINES OF A POEM BY DAWSON

Prior Claims

As the fur traders went about discovering for themselves the Peace River Country, it was, of course, already occupied. The first Natives of the Peace to be encountered by the Europeans were the Kenistenoag — the People of the Woods. On the French Canadian tongue this became Kristeneaux, and later simply Kris. The English, therefore, called them Cree.

The Cree met the Hudson's Bay Co. traders in the first years of the trade, and learned early the White Man's ways. This knowledge and the trade goods they acquired gave the Cree power over their neighbours. They became the dominant tribe in the Northwest.

In those days the Cree were a handsome race — a fact not unnoticed by the observant Mackenzie.

> *"Of all the Nations I have seen on the continent, the Kristeneaux women are the most comely. Their figure is generally well-proportioned, and the regularity of their features would be acknowledged by the more civilized people of Europe."*

Beautiful women aside, it was a hard life for the Cree. Starvation was a constant threat during the winter months. Families were often immobilized and isolated from help, depending on their luck and the random moose for sustenance. In the Peace forests there was not the seemingly inexhaustible buffalo herd that supported the Plains Indian.

The Woodland Cree lived in small units of one or two families so as to optimize their unpredictable food supply, and the large group ceremony was not common. Instead of ritual, the Cree developed a strong communion with nature. When destiny hung on the changing wind, it was important to maintain good relations with the spirits of so whimisical a force — more important than being seen at group ceremony. This spiritual communion was seen by their neighbours as supernatural power, which only added to the Cree's reputation as warriors (a reputation garnered chiefly from facility with European weaponry).

Legend claims that at some early date the Cree were

asked by the fur traders to describe their neighbours to the west — neighbours whom the traders were preparing to meet. Not wishing to hurt their own expectations, the Cree painted a picture of their neighbours that left the Europeans with only one conclusion — the tribe in question must be slaves. From this description has come the names for the Slave Lakes.

Eventually the traders made their way westward and met this new people. When asked for their own version of their name, they replied that they were "Dene" — the Chosen People. This was too vague for the traders. They were more interested in the name the Dene gave to their river — Tsades, which, after all, was what they were here for. The Europeans decided to call the

ABOVE: A Beaver family. RIGHT: With teepees from the Plains Indians, canvas tents from the White traders, and cotton and wool from England, a Native family attempts to adjust and survive in the changing Peace Country. OPPOSITE: A Cree warrior.

Natives by the name of their river — the Beaver! For the Europeans, the name of the river would remain the Peace.

The Beaver were a quiet and reserved tribe. Unlike the Cree, they wanted little to do with the newcomers. They were, said an early traveller, a peaceable and quiet people, and perhaps the most honest of any on the face of the earth.

They strongly discouraged the practice of intermarriage with the White Man, so common among the Cree. It was a policy initiated as a remedy to abuse, which may in fact have contributed to the Beaver's most unfortunate history.

All the tribes of the north suffered severely the effects of the European diseases, especially smallpox. The Beaver were decimated. It is possible that some immunity to these ravages would have been supplied with a mixing of bloodlines through intermarriage.

During the 1800's other elements of Old World culture, for the most part less destructive, made their way to the Peace tribes. Catholic, Anglican and Methodist missions provided a new system of worship to complement a rudimentary education, and crude facilities for the practice of the healing arts. The Cree and the Beaver became progressively more civilized as the century did, adopting European clothing, language and values. Life began to revolve around the European institutions of Church and trading post.

At the close of that century, leather and fur from the forest had been replaced by cotton and wool from England. The spirits of "Watigo," the cannibal monster, and "Pakakos," the flying skeleton, had been replaced as well, by the Father, Son, and Holy Ghost. Even so, the Indians of the Peace were not prepared for the world that was rudely thrust upon them.

In 1898 the Peace Country played host to some of the more crass and self-seeking elements of civilization, as Klondike gold fever swept north. The Native popu-

Treaty No. 8 is signed.
"Do you not allow the Indians to make their own
conditions, so that they may benefit as much as
possible? Why I say this is that we today make
arrangements that are to last as long as the sun shines
and the water runs."
CREE SPOKESMAN KEENOOSHAYO

lations were abused and trampled on. Unlike the traders and the priests, these intruders had little use for so childlike a people. The Indians were horrified by the strangers' conduct.

A year later a treaty commission was sent into the Peace to try to remedy the situation. Following precedent established in agreements with the Plains Indians, Treaty #8 offered those who wished to continue being regarded Indian special status within the confines of newly established reserves. Those who decided to throw in their lot with the White Man were given scrip for 160 acres of farm land.

Although the propriety of this solution has been laid open to question through the years, there has never been any question of its expediency. With the signing of Treaty #8 the land was freed for the plough and an age of innocence was lost.

By allowing the scrip to be instantly negotiable, the commissioners ensured that most of it would find its way to the Whites – at bargain prices.

ABOVE: *Catholic mission at Lesser Slave Lake –
1906.* RIGHT: *Appearing here as an apparition,
Emile Grouard was in reality a most common figure
in the Peace Country. He came to Quebec from France
when twenty, entered the priesthood, and two years
later in 1862 entered the Peace. His early ministry
took him from Dawson City to Edmonton, and for the
most part he would travel those thousands of miles
alone, possibly more miles than anyone else of his era.
Certainly it was a long journey. It lasted 69 years, as
priest and then Bishop of Athabasca, during which
time he made tremendous contributions to both the
spiritual and temporal needs of Native and newcomer.
He died at the age of 91, in the town that took his
name, Grouard.*

Gold

It was the Summer of 1897 and the American steamer Portland slowly made her way down the coast from Alaska to Seattle. On that voyage, her cabins were the constant scene of merrymaking while her vault overflowed with more than a million in gold. It was the confirmation that everyone had been waiting for — the news that would torment and tantalize and send men packing from as far away as Europe. The Klondike Gold Rush had begun.

Fortunes were made and fortunes lost. For every dream fulfilled, ten were broken. Those who made the trek without knowledge of the Arctic, or respect for its demands, were glad to trade their dreams for sourdough, for salt pork, or for a little warmth. Stubborn to the end, others went on to their desserts, an empty gold-pan clutched in frozen hope, filled only with desire.

The Peace Country played host to many of those who set out for the Klondike — the ones who mistakenly assumed that the shortest route (from Edmonton through the Peace overland) would also be the most convenient. Some had read Dr. Dawson's report of an overland trip he had made to the Yukon in which he had downplayed the hardships and his own consumate skill, thereby giving the impression that there was nothing to it. Others found maps that portrayed an almost total lack of information about the North, insisting for example, that the Rockies ended just north of Jasper, or that the distance from Edmonton to Dawson City was but a few hundred miles. Armed with misinformation they set out to do battle with a climate and terrain unknown and unforgiving.

For the Peace Country, the most significant aspect of the Klondike Rush was the exposure it gave to this mysterious land. When the gold panned out, many of the miners who had crossed through the Peace came back to investigate the verdant prairie they had noticed in their journey. Some stayed, and some told others.

The Jessie and her crew await the lucky breeze that blows North.

The barrels were filled with rice, beans and other cereals, most of which spread out on the trail – a few miles out of Edmonton.

LEFT: *A hint of hardship to come?*
BELOW LEFT: *Prospects look good for this little stern-wheeler.*
BELOW RIGHT: *"This here's an American caynoo."*

AUG. 1897.

OPPOSITE AND ABOVE: In Edmonton they said she was the first lady to enter the Klondike. Actually Mrs. Garner's party never got farther than Spirit River, 200 miles out of Edmonton. The outfitter-guide they had hired in California "vamoosed," taking their grub-stake with him.

A.M. Bezanson

It was a Klondike adventurer who caught the ear of A.M. Bezanson, destined to be one of the Peace Country's biggest boosters.

Bezanson was born in Nova Scotia in 1878 (Dawson was just about to cross the Rockies and enter the Peace Country). As a young man he roamed the American Midwest offering his services to homesteaders looking for land. By 1906 the Midwest was settled. When mention of the Peace River's agricultural possibilities was made to him, Bezanson realized a new challenge. He packed his kit and headed Northwest!

For someone traveling light, the water route up the Lesser Slave River from Athabasca Landing, then across the Lesser Slave Lake, was the easiest route into the Peace Country. At Athabasca Landing Bezanson was forced to wait six weeks while a new steamboat was completed and tested. He employed himself in painting the Revillon Freres buildings, and thereby became acquainted with a party of Revillon executives, themselves conducting the young heir to the company fortunes on his first visit to Canada. Bezanson was able to travel in style, for the best part of the summer, with the Revillon people.

He got as far as the Fort St. John area that year, and then headed back to Edmonton, snapping pictures with his Kodak, and marvelling at the panorama before him.

During the following winter Bezanson developed his snapshots and word sketches into a small book on the Peace Country. The Edmonton Journal, just starting at that time, agreed to publish 5,000 copies of "Peace River Trail."

The book was a success. The Federal Government took 1,000 copies for foreign distribution. The rest were sold by the newspaper and by Bezanson himself, who loaded a wagon with them and headed East for Winnipeg. Interest in the book, and in the Peace, spread by word of mouth, and the Edmonton Journal received mail-orders from as far away as China.

No land schemes indeed...

FOREWORD

"I hear the tread of Nations yet to be,
The first low wash of waves where soon shall roll a human sea ;
The ashes of an Empire here are plastic yet and warm,
The chaos of a mighty world is rounding into form."

THIS book is offered not merely as an advertising medium, but to meet the demand of the ever-increasing multitude of home-seekers for information about the still unoccupied and undeveloped areas of fertile land suitable for ranching and agricultural purposes, which lie in districts so remote as to render it next to impossible for the Government Land Department to have acquired sufficient authentic information — for free distribution – to meet the requirements of those who desire to leave the well-beaten path and lead the army of invasion into this practically unknown, but most highly favored, part of the Last West.

The writer spent the summer of 1906 travelling through the most fertile portions of this vast area, gathering the most reliable information obtainable from the few inhabitants now there, and using his eyes and his camera to the best of his ability. The results are given herewith, with the sincere hope that beneficial information, if not entertainment, may be gleaned therefrom.

I have tried to avoid exaggeration in any form and have made no statements but those which, either from personal knowledge or from the experience of responsible men long in the country, I believe to be the truth. Nor am I interested in any land or colonization scheme. I was, however, so thoroughly captivated by this new Land of Promise, that I expect to make it my future home, and I desire to assist in pointing out the trail to others that I may not lack for company.

Edmonton, Alberta
May 1st, 1907

A. M. BEZANSON

When the ice broke in the Spring, Bezanson was ready to go North again. This time he was armed with a copy of Dr. Dawson's report of 1879, which made recommendations for a feasible rail route through the region. Bezanson was convinced, after reading the report, and finding surveyors' stakes on the banks of the river, that the railroad would cross the Smoky river at its junction with the Simonette.

The next few years in Bezanson's life serve well to illustrate the social order of life in the pioneer era. He set about to build a homestead for himself and he mentions a blacksmith he met near Grande Prairie while working on this project. The blacksmith was so busy with his trade that he had no time to go out to Edmonton for supplies (a return trip of three months). The blacksmith therefore asked Bezanson if he would find

RIGHT AND OPPOSITE: Gentlemen competitors at Athabasca "none of the bloodletting ...of ye olden days."

for him a woman — a wife — on his next trip to the city.

Bezanson found it hard to take the request seriously, and suggested that he would not be able to make the proper choice for someone else, not having been able to make one for himself. This did not faze the blacksmith, who was apparently quite willing to accept whatever Bezanson was able to come up with!

There was no wife for the blacksmith on Bezanson's next trip out, but he did find one for himself — an Eastern woman of some standing, who was as fascinated by the pioneer experience as she was ignorant of it.

Together they built their homestead and made their plans, though for her they were never more than plans. She died giving birth to their child, many days journey from the nearest hospital.

These are the Revillon buildings two years after Bezanson painted them.

A WORD TO HOMESEEKERS

The Hudson's Bay Company and Revillon Brothers, Limited, have stores at all the trading posts mentioned in this book, which are well stocked, transportation facilities considered, and where the traveller may purchase necessary supplies at a fair price, and be sure of receiving courteous treatment. To add to the convenience of travellers, each of those companies have a letter of credit system whereby one may, before starting, deposit a sum of money sufficient to cover the expense of a trip through that country and receive a letter of credit good for

H. B. Co's Store, Hudson's Hope

transportation, supplies or cash at any of their trading posts, a plan very much to be preferred to carrying a large sum of money on one's person while on such a trip. Those who do not care to undertake the trip through the Last West entirely upon their own resources can arrange for transportation, supplies, etc., with either of those companies, and place themselves completely in their charge, with the assurance that the best accommodation procurable will be at their disposal.

Revillon Brothers, Limited, though they have only been engaged in the fur trade in the Last West a short time, have practically unlimited capital at their disposal, well equipped trading posts in charge of competent men, and are doing business on a scale which has placed them on a par with the great Hudson's Bay Company.

While there is naturally a keen business competition between these two companies, there is none of the blood-letting spirit which characterized the fur-traders of ye olden days.

Romance had proved to be a costly pastime for Bezanson, but as all pioneers must, he was willing to live with reality. There was an infant, and he needed a mother. Bezanson's first wife's sister accepted the role of both mother and wife.

The homestead was completed, but now Bezanson had launched himself in a new dream, the building and promotion of a townsite — the town of Bezanson.

He prepared a pamphlet on the subject:

"Bezanson is not a sub-division. It is a town-site. It is beautifully situated at about one hundred and twenty feet above the river of which it commands a magnificent view... we intend to carry out the wide streets for streetcars every four blocks in the business section."

He may have been dreaming, but he was not wasting

Davidson is the front seat passenger. Bezanson sits behind the driver. The fur coat was a good idea, just the thing for open winter touring, it also made an excellent traction mat when spread under the rear wheels.

time. He recruited a sales agent in Vancouver, and together they began to sell the project, lot by lot. Enthusiastic support came from Mackenzie and Mann of the Canadian Northern Railway, who assured all who would listen that a line through the Peace along the route that Bezanson proposed was about to begin at any time — at any time that Governments chose to finance it.

In 1913 Bezanson secured more publicity for his project by driving the first automobile into the Peace. Now he was trying to enlist the support of A.J. Davidson, a well-known Edmonton land promoter.

Davidson would not support what he could not see, but felt that he was "too old and soft" for the hike in by normal methods of transport. Bezanson took the older man, and his 1911 Cadillac, over the Edson Trail and into the Peace country on a trip of two thousand miles. Bezanson describes the look on the faces of the school children (and some of their teachers) when confronted by their first automobile. He also describes the look on Davidson's face as they race across Lesser Slave Lake at 65 miles an hour in order to keep ahead of the breaking ice left in their wake!

Despite all his efforts, the Town of Bezanson never materialized. When the Railroad did cross the Smoky (1916) it did so many miles downstream, and the buildings that had been erected were eventually razed:

"They left the well-holes and the cellars, that was all."

Yet A.M. Bezanson went on. He possessed the sort of temperament that is fulfilled in action; the sort of temperament that has pursued triumph and tragedy throughout the history of the Western World, even to the Peace Country, or as Bezanson called it, "The Last West." He was criticized as a heartless speculator by those who had invested in his townsite, but no one lost more than did Bezanson, himself the founder of the dream.

He was also a talented writer. His early efforts can be found included in this book, as samples from "Peace River Trail." Nearly fifty years later, Bezanson was to write his autobiography, "Sodbusters Invade the Peace." Despite the title, the book offers a smoothly written and fascinating look at the life of an outstanding Canadian adventurer from a Peace River Past.

Ways and Means

Before our modern age, there were two modes of transport open to the traveler in the Peace Country. There was travel by land, which was obvious, and travel by water, which was sensible.

For land travel there were carts and wagons and sleighs of every description, and these were conveyed along tracks and trails by a surprising variety of four-legged beast, including almost anything that was even marginally agreeable to the task. When these could not be found, or not afforded, there was always the two-legged variety.

In the light of our modern expectation, descriptions of land travel in the Peace are often a horror to imagine, and assuredly, they were a horror to endure. For example, there was the Edson Trail.

Edson is due west of Edmonton, and almost due south of Grande Prairie. When the railroad was completed from Edmonton as far as Edson, the latter became an obvious jumping-off point for settlers going into the Peace. It was the shortest route.

But distance is better measured in time than in space, at least with regard to the Edson Trail. When the federal government put through the Trail in 1911, they opened a path of some two hundred miles, through bogs and marshes, and up and down ridiculously steep grades which were all but impassible, and even then, only at certain times of the year.

The trip took ten days in either direction. There was not a single roadhouse along the way, and everything required for man and beast was taken along, or done without. In many places the hills were too steep for the team approaching them to negotiate, in which case a forced rest was called until the next team happened along, at which time both teams could be hitched to one cart. It was a rest of varied duration.

More than a few expectant souls were left confounded by another unhappy circumstance, the arrival of an early spring! The most popular time to travel on the Edson Trail was in late winter, when the snow still provided ease of movement, but in time for a full sea-

Crossing the Peace at Dunvegan, settlers head for Grande Prairie.

son of warm weather in which to settle in after arrival. Warm winds off the mountains were as unpredictable as they were unwelcome. What was one day a sleigh trail, was reduced, on the next, to mud. The weary teamster was forced to unload his conveyance, remove its runners, and re-fit it with wheels, assuming he was possessed of them.

But there were opportunities on the Trail. It was unusual for the incoming settler not to be solicited by at least one returnee, who, having given up further down the line, was looking to relieve himself of his possessions, often only for the price of a rail ticket back to civilization. The persevering traveler might emerge at the far end of the Edson Trail in most sorry circumstance, but his spirit would soon soar in the welcome suspicion that the worst must be over.

As usual, there was a better way. In exchange for the mud and mosquitoes of the bush, there was the romance and civility of the river boats. As the well informed wayfarer knew, the best way to go was by water.

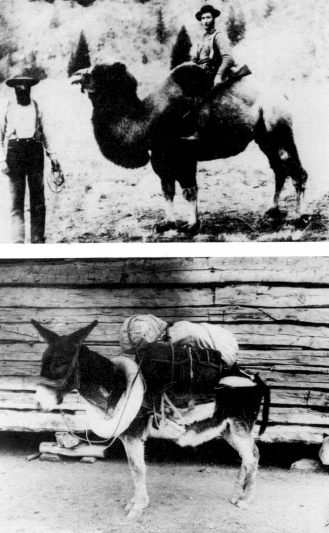

"A surprising variety..."

First Lady of the Peace, the D.A. Thomas
Paddles her way upstream
While red roofs mark her passage.

A perfect fitting of function to form, the birch bark canoe was the universal mode of water transport in almost all of Canada when Mackenzie adopted it. The materials for its construction were available everywhere, and although strong enough to carry thousands of pounds, it was light enough to be itself carried by one or two men.

When the North West Company ventured over the Rockies to British Columbia, they found dug-outs and cedar strip canoes. There was very little birch on the West Coast. But they were so attached to their birch bark canoes, a trader reported, that "the country was ransacked for prime birch bark more often than for prime furs; and to guard against a failure in this fanciful article, a stock of it was shipped at Montreal for London, and from thence conveyed around Cape Horn..."

When the Hudson's Bay Company joined the river trade, it favoured the larger and more stable York boats. Their lack of speed and agility was deemed a reasonable exchange for much improved cargo handling capacities, both as regards volume and also its safe conveyance. The flat-oared York boats became a common sight on the Peace River in the last half of the Nineteenth Century. But the golden age of navigation on the Peace was still to come.

"Largest steamboat to ply the Canadian inland waters"

It may have been a small exaggeration on the part of local newsmen, but the D.A. Thomas was by all means the largest passenger ship to venture on the Peace. Her hull measured 161 feet x 37 feet, and when she was launched in 1916, she carried cabin accommodation for 160 travelers. As well, there were staterooms with electricity and hot and cold running water. She boasted the finest in linen and silverware, and there were parlours for both ladies and gentlemen.

The age of steam had come to the Peace some thirty-five years before. The little steamer S.S. Grahame made the three hundred mile run down the Athabasca and Slave Rivers, and then two hundred miles back up the Peace to the Vermilion Chutes.

From there, canoes and scows were employed to move goods further up the river. Not surprisingly, the Grahame was owned and operated by the Hudson's Bay Company, who enjoyed a monopoly on river traffic until 1903, when they were challenged from a most unlikely quarter — The Oblate Order of Mary Immaculate!

The Oblate Missions, under Bishop Emile Grouard, were among the largest contributors to early life in the Peace. They had been providing their own needs in river transport for years, but as more settlers took up the call of the North, the far-sighted Bishop purchased, at Peterborough, Ontario, the parts for a sixty-foot screw-driven passenger boat, which, when assembled at Shaftsbury, near the present town of Peace River, would offer a somewhat sporadic but improved service on the Peace until 1911. The little steamer — the St. Charles — with Father LeTreste at the wheel, became a local fixture.

*From paddle to oar to paddle-wheel – three ages of
travel on the river.*

Early work on the D.A. Thomas at Peace River – 1915. The boilers and hardware came from Edmonton. Everything else was made to order – on the spot.

Peace river – Hudson's Hope: $35.00 going up; $20.00 coming down.

Anticipating oil production in the Peace, the D.A. Thomas was fitted with tanks to transport it.

James Cornwall – "Peace River Jim"

Born in Brantford Ontario in 1869, he had seen much of the world as a merchant sailor by the time he was twenty-five. Cornwall came North with the Klondike fever, but realized quickly that the best opportunities were closer at hand, in the just opening Peace Country. In turn he contracted to carry the mail, trapped and traded, built and operated steamboats, and promoted mining, railroads and settlement. Between 1908 and 1912 Cornwall was the Liberal member of the Alberta Legislature, representing Peace River. "Somebody has always got to go ahead," he was quoted as saying. "Someone's been doing it since the world began."

If there was a challenge to their supremacy on the river, the Company of Adventurers would prove again, as they had done so often in the past, that they were up to it. In quick time plans were drawn and spruce was cut for a real river boat. With a cargo capacity of eighty tons, and accomodation for twenty-five passengers, the 110 foot sternwheeler Peace River was launched from Fort Vermilion in time for the 1905 navigation season. The men of the Bay were back on top.

Traffic increased, and others began to contemplate a share of the business on the Peace. 1911 saw the formation of the Peace River Trading and Land Company (known as the Diamond "P"), and the launching by that company of the Grenfell. However, that company's rivalry was short lived. The Grenfell burned after three short years of service, and the Diamond "P" went into voluntary liquidation.

Peace River Jim Cornwall was among those who chartered the Peace River Navigation Company in 1915. This company operated The Northland Call for a few seasons on the upper river, never with a profit. A much more serious effort was launched by The Peace River Development Company Corp. and its founder, Lord Rhondda, David A. Thomas.

The D.A. Thomas was part of a strategy to augment river traffic with a railroad from Prince Albert to Kitimat, oil and coal development, and a radio telegraph system to link the North. The Thomas was fitted with storage tanks for the transport of the oil. But first the Great War hampered their plans, and then the untimely death of their visionary leader.

But at least part of their dream carried on. The D.A. Thomas plied the waters of the Peace for many years (until 1930) offering a convenience that was appreciated by all. It was only fitting that this first lady of the Peace should end her days under the guidance of the people who started it all — the Hudson's Bay Company!

They made them from wood, and wood made them go!

Big and black and brawny,
The Iron Horse comes late to the Peace.
Here the GTP locomotive puffs and snorts,
Waiting for her masters
To pull the throttles hard.

*Tiny hamlets flourish
briefly as wooded tracts
yield to railway steel...*

*...while further up the
line, workers pause for the
ever-curious camera.*

Transportation in the new century was not to remain an elegant affair. Serenity would have to make room for a new form of efficiency as steel rails crawled north on spikes and ties. It was the dawn of new potentials. Where before men went where the river went, now they could go where they chose.

Yet choice is not conceived in a vacuum, and the more important the choice, the more likely it will be accompanied by politics. In choosing rail routes through the Peace, decisions were dictated as often by politicians as they were by common sense. This state of affairs may have best been illustrated by the rail route that never came to pass.

Building the grade at Peace River.

Routes through the Peace had been a source of speculation ever since the time of Dawson's first suggestions in the 1870's. He argued for a northern route through the Rockies on the basis that it would be an aid to prosperous settlement, whereas a southern route would have to pass through hundreds of miles of barren land. However, the southern route was shorter, and the C.P.R. went through Calgary and the Kicking Horse Pass.

By 1910 many elements of the equation had changed. All the good homestead lands to the south had been settled and the good people of Edmonton were clamouring for a line through the northern Prairies, through their city, and then on to the Coast. It was logical for the settlers in the Peace Country to kindle new hope.

That hope burned bright as it was learned that not one, but two lines were being built through Edmonton. The Grand Trunk Pacific emerged on the northern prairies just ahead of the Canadian Northern and both arrived in Edmonton on top of one another. The Grand Trunk announced it would head north to the Peace country, and cross the mountains by the Pine Pass.

Surveyors were dispatched amid fanfare, while rival Canadian Northern officials congratulated themselves on their wiser choice of the Yellowhead Pass through the Rockies. Now they could pursue it at their own pace. But once out of Edmonton and the public eye, those Grand Trunk surveyors quickly abandoned the Peace and swung down to the route they had been secretly ordered to survey all along — the Yellowhead.

So it came to pass that both lines went through the Yellowhead. The Grand Trunk Pacific got its survey to Ottawa sooner and was able to secure the most favourable grades and crossings along the route. The Canadian Northern, asleep at the switch, was left with all the costly excavations. The Peace country remained without a railroad.

Eventually a railroad did enter the Peace, but its progress was depressingly slow. In 1916 the Edmonton Dunvegan and B.C. Railroad left Edmonton with a mandate to link the Peace country to the West Coast. It was a promise kept, though it required a Provincial Government take-over and another forty years. Only then did rails run from the Peace to salt water.

Bridge-work completed, the E.D.& B.C. brings a new age of steam to Peace River. Now just a long day's journey out of Edmonton, (when everything was on track), the Peace Country finally entered the Twentieth Century.

The Settlers

Railways and automobiles, radios and telephones, and the Panama Canal — the Twentieth Century excited the imagination. Victoria was gone, and the Canadian Prime Minister claimed the new century for Canada. Optimism ran high in all parts of the Country, including the Peace.

...One day Canyon City may rank among the foremost cities of the Great West...a beautiful city spread out over the valley...the streets being laid out in such a way that takes advantage of the natural configuration of the ground...to the east are numerous great factories, for the immense power of the water in the canyon has been harnessed...railways radiate from here in all directions...a non-stop aeroplane runs daily to Winnipeg, to Chicago, and to Vancouver... there are many other large cities in this northern country, and the rivalry between Canyon City and Dunvegan is great.

Written for a British readership in 1912, the description of "Canyon City" was ambitious, but also somewhat propehetic. However, a few years after it was written, the residents decided they would be more comfortable with their former name — Hudson's Hope.

Perhaps the mood was best summed up by Viscount Rhondda (D.A. Thomas):

"How the imagination can play over that ...wonderful virgin tract, with its lakes and rivers and mountains, its auriferious valleys ...its visions of smiling fields and comfortable homesteads and thriving ports and ships going to and from the ends of the earth."

Thomas died during the First War — before he could bring many of his plans for those wonderful virgin tracts into being.

The West had filled up. By the turn of the century there was no more first quality land to be had for homesteading on the Prairies. It was the end of an era in Canadian history.

Yet beyond the forest belt that starts near Edmonton, and east of the Rockies, the Peace River Country had remained virtually untouched by the plow. Despite the recommendation of men like Dawson, the

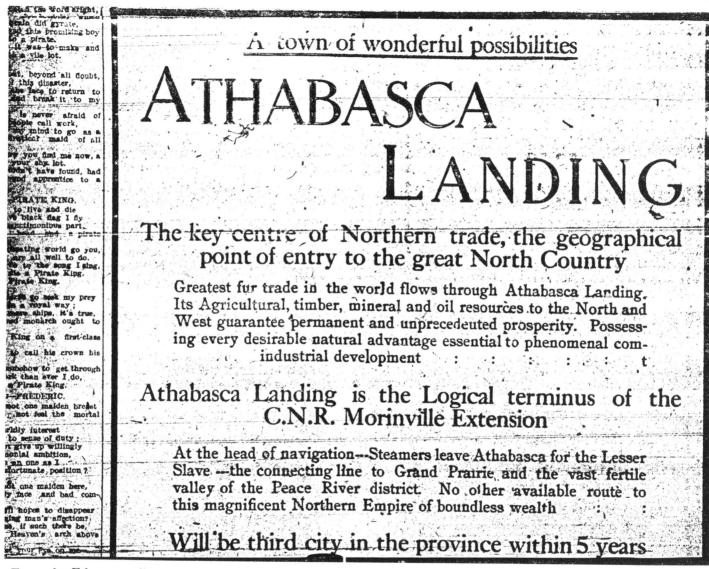

From the Edmonton Journal, 1907.

agricultural possibilities of the Peace were still questioned, though even the questioning was discouraged.

Then in 1907, the Federal Government finally took responsibility for the Peace River Block — three and a half million acres on the B.C. side.

Newspapers in Edmonton and Vancouver began to pick up the theme. Articles debated the agricultural potential while advertisements tempted the small investor to gamble on Peace River land — a sure thing, they claimed, at any price.

But there were no sure things, and the price was paid by the pioneers — the men and women who entered the Peace with only their hopes and dreams and a couple of steamer trunks. Most came fuelled by adventure, some were driven by desperation, but all were prepared to take a chance.

For the Guest family, pictured on the cover of this book, optimism was surely underscored by trepidation — a romantic picture framed in all the realities of hardship. In a wagon filled with all their family belongings, they set out in early spring on a journey that would take months, searching for a piece of land that could mean a new life. They slept in canvas tents and hoped there would be enough time to build a cabin before winter set in.

Mr. Guest could not know what lay before him. In Edmonton (where the picture was taken) he would be told by some that the Peace was too far north for farming, and that the soil was poor. In Toronto and Montreal people rode in automobiles and street cars. In New York and London there were subways, while great

TEXT CONTINUES ON PAGE 95

THE EDMO

VOL. 4, No. 102

A New Rich Area in Peace River

Three Million Acres Held by the Dominion Along British Columbia are Full of Possibilities

(Special to The Journal)

Ottawa, Mar. 12.—The report of John A. McDonnell, C. E., on the delimitation of three and a half million acres in the Peace River country, which passed over to the Dominion in 1884, was presented to parliament yesterday. The work has been in progress for the past two years. The selected area runs north and south eighty miles, and east and west sixty-eight miles, twenty-eight chains. Peace River was taken as the basis of the survey, and commencing where the British Columbia boundary crosses the river the line was run due north along the boundary for the distance of forty-six and a half miles, and then south from the Peace River along the boundary thirty-three and a half miles, thus giving the total length of eighty miles.

MacDonnell says the soil is a yellow clay loam, capable of growing all classes of cereals and vegetables. The survey party fully tested the fertility of the soil. The potatoes raised, MacDonnel said, were the finest he ever saw in his life. Out of four bushels of specially picked potatoes the majority ran seven pounds each. The distribution of water in the new area is stated to be not sufficient for the requirements of a large settlement. The timber consists of poplar, spruce, birch, and alder, all of which were undersized. Coal in abundance was found.

The climate is enjoyable, the summers not being too hot, nor the winters so cold as in Manitoba and Ontario. There is a liability to early frosts, but the surveyors think they will disappear with settlement and cultivation. MacDonnell does not recommend settlers to go into the country until railway accommodation is afforded.

Constant toil supplants naive faith. It took courage to dig in and to remain.

*Growth of a town: Peace
River Landing in 1912...*

...and as the town of Peace River five years later.

The strains and sweat of man and beast
Break prairie's hard brown soil.

"The nicest way, for the experienced traveler who desires to see the country, is on horseback, with one packhorse to the man. The native horses, when properly used, will require no further feed than that which groes in plenty everywhere."
PEACE RIVER TRAIL, A.M. BEZANSON

liners plied the ocean between them.

Back East they would not understand Mr. Guest — his was a pioneer spirit.

But the pioneers did find support. Governments were finally encouraging settlement. Many of those who opposed it were now on reserves, and the fur trading interests realized that with Governments involved, there was a big business in settlers' supplies.

Surveys were completed, and industrial investments earmarked. Publicity campaigns and promotions were launched across the Dominion, and reached around the world.

They were heady days, but already on a far horizon loomed the stark reality of an older troubled world — one that demanded resolution, and could not be escaped.

The young and strong were trained to kill and then sent away to die. Those who returned brought with them a disillusion that would take a generation to dispel.

But then, veterans returning from the trenches looked westward for new hope, as far from the old world as they could be. Of these, some had heard mentioned the name of a new land in the Northwest. They came looking not for gold or furs, nor any other riches; they came looking only for a name, and the promise that it held for them — the Promise of the Peace.

The First World War ended an age of innocence in Canada at the same time as it heralded a new sophistication in the world at large — a new awareness that would not manifest itself before a cruel depression and another ugly war had been suffered.

The Pioneer Era in Canada ends here. At the very end of that era ends the Peace River Past — A Canadian Adventure.

Credits

Hudson's Bay Company: Pages 1, 22, 83 Top Left, 83 Top Right; Provincial Archives of Alberta, Edward Brown Collection: Pages 3, 11, 25, 26, 41, 46 Top, 46 Bottom, 47 Bottom Left, 47 Bottom Right, 48, 49 Right, 49 Left, 54, 55, 61 Bottom, 86, 90 Bottom, 91; Provincial Archives of Alberta, H. Pollard Collection: Page 83 Bottom; Provincial Archives of Alberta: Pages 44 Right, 57, 63, 65, 66 Top, 66 Bottom, 67, 71, 74, 82, 87 Top, 87 Bottom, 89, 90 Top, 93; Glenbow Archives: Pages 14, 40 Top, 47 Top, 68, 72 Top, 72 Bottom, 73, 75, 94; RCMP Museum: Pages 42, 43 Top, 43 Bottom; Vancouver Public Library: Pages 16, 29, 61 Top; Province of Manitoba Archives: Page 40 Bottom: Province of Ontario Archives: Page 17; National Gallery of Canada, Canadian War Memorials Collection: Page 15; Provincial Archives of British Columbia: Pages 20, 33, 35, 36, 37; Public Archives of Canada: Pages 12 (C21789), 34 (PA74675), 44 Left (C30269), 60 (PA29833), 69 (PA29842), 80 Top Left (PA38567), Top Right (PA17369), Bottom (PA18689), 95 (PA22995). Material on Pages 53, 56, 86 ©Copyright A.M. Bezanson, 1907, from Peace River Trail by A.M. Bezanson, reprinted by permission of J.R. Bezanson.

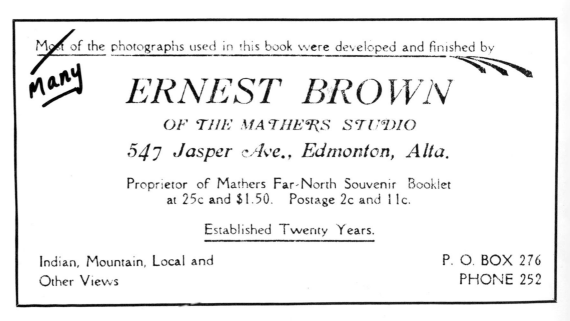